CAREERS IN SEARCH AND RESCUE OPERATIONS

Careers in
FIRE DEPARTMENTS'
SEARCH AND RESCUE UNITS

Mitchell Fall

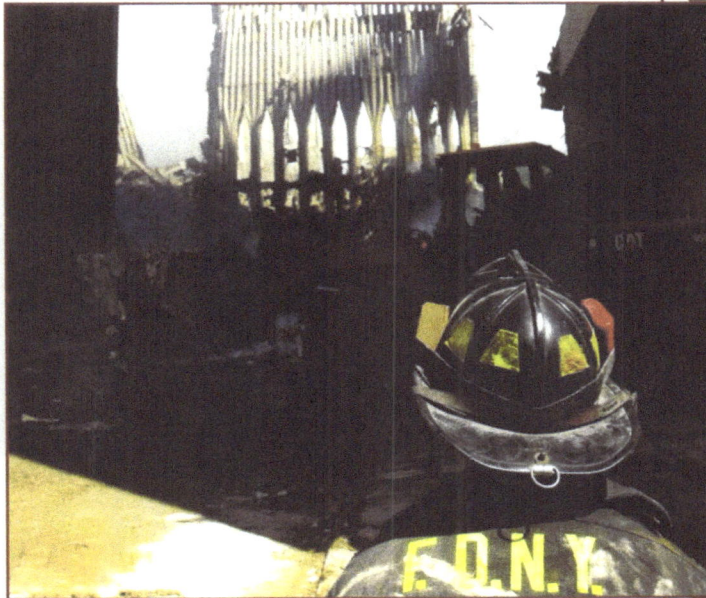

the rosen publishing group's
**rosen
central**

To the memory of Jed Sommers, who loved playing fireman

Published in 2003 by The Rosen Publishing Group, Inc.
29 East 21st Street, New York, NY 10010

First Edition

Library of Congress Cataloging-in-Publication Data

Fall, Mitchell.
Careers in fire departments' search and rescue units / Mitchell Fall.
    p. cm. — (Careers in search and rescue operations)
Summary: Discusses the history of search and rescue work by fire departments, requirements of becoming a fire fighter, and the roles various fire departments played after the events of September 11, 2001.
Includes bibliographical references and index.
ISBN: 978-1-4358-9060-2
1. Fire extinction—Vocational guidance—Juvenile literature. 2. Lifesaving at fires—Vocational guidance—Juvenile literature. 3. Search and rescue operations—Vocational guidance—Juvenile literature. [1. Fire extinction—Vocational guidance. 2. Rescue work—Vocational guidance. 3. Vocational guidance.] I. Title. II. Series.
TH9119 .F35 2003
363.37'8—dc21

                                                        2002013173

Manufactured in the United States of America

CONTENTS

INTRODUCTION

One Day in September

September 11, 2001. It is a beautiful autumn morning in New York City. Two French brothers, Jules and Gedeon Naudet, are filming a documentary about firefighters. From behind the camera, Jules captures firefighters checking a gas leak in lower Manhattan. He then shifts the camera upward and, by chance, captures an airplane just as it slams into the north tower of the World Trade Center, one of the two tallest buildings in New York and the second largest in the United States. It is 8:46 in the morning. As the tower bursts into flames, Jules and the firefighters rush to the scene of the largest man-made disaster in U.S. history.

At the north tower, the firefighters quickly set up a command post close to the burning building. Although they move with speed and precision, their hearts sink as the vastness of the tragedy and their mission become clear. Then come the awful thumps, one after another—the sounds of people jumping from the floors above the flames and landing amid the rubble.

The south tower of the World Trade Center crumbles to the ground after terrorists crashed an airplane into the building on September 11, 2001. More than 300 firefighters died trying to save people who were inside the World Trade Center.

FIRE DEPARTMENT

Members of Rescue Company 1, a team of Manhattan fire-fighters specially trained to deal with emergency search and rescue operations, enter the north tower. While thousands of people rush down the stairs, these brave firefighters ascend toward the flames in search of trapped victims. The oxygen tanks on their backs and hoses and tools in their hands add 60 pounds (27.2 kilograms) to their already substantial load. The heat generated by the fire is extraordinary. Not one of these members from Rescue 1 will make it out alive.

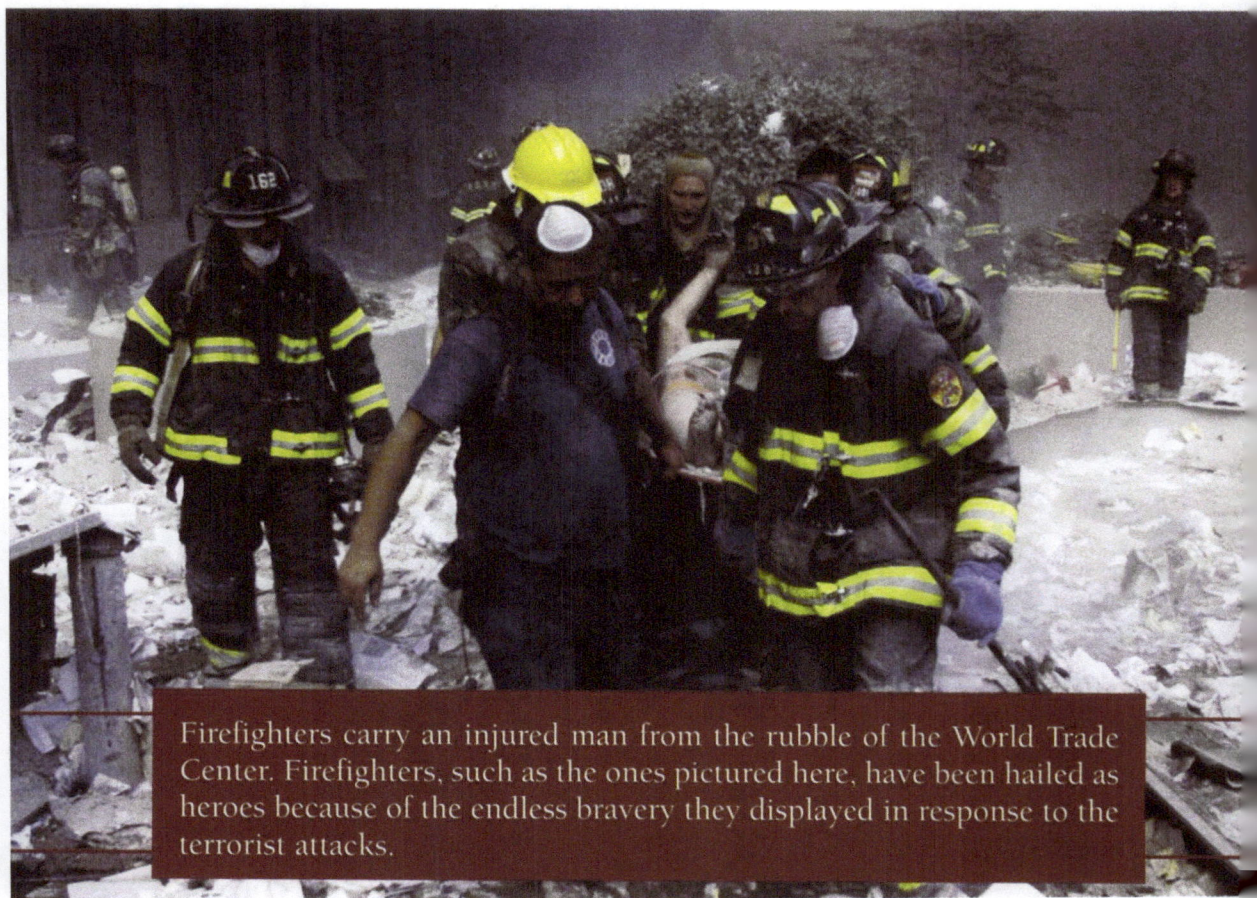

Firefighters carry an injured man from the rubble of the World Trade Center. Firefighters, such as the ones pictured here, have been hailed as heroes because of the endless bravery they displayed in response to the terrorist attacks.

Amid the horror and chaos, Jules Naudet's camera keeps rolling. It records the buzz and sudden bang of a second airplane crashing into the World Trade Center's south tower. It later registers the collapse of the south tower and the panic of people running for shelter.

The Naudet brothers' final two-hour documentary film captures the mixture of fear, courage, and grace under pressure that was exhibited by the hundreds of firefighters who were the first to arrive at the scene of the September 11 disaster.

These "first respondents"—most from the Fire Department of New York (FDNY)—immediately went to work fighting the scorching flames and searching for survivors. The conditions they were working in were chaotic. The air was thick with dust and toxic fumes, and the ground was a mess of rubble. Thousands of sheets of paper from the towers' offices blew around like leaves.

All in all, 343 firefighters died that day sacrificing their lives for others. It is estimated that at least 25,000 people were safely evacuated from the World Trade Center complex by emergency rescue workers on September 11. Without the many firefighters who responded so quickly and courageously, it is certain that many more lives would have been lost.

CHAPTER 1

To the Rescue

The history of fire fighting in the United States dates back almost four centuries. In 1607, the first permanent English settlement of Jamestown was founded in Virginia. Less than a year later, the small community suffered its first fire: a raging inferno that destroyed most of the new settlers' homes. In the online magazine Firehouse.com, the commander of Jamestown, Captain James Smith, had this to say about the disaster: "I begin to think that it is safer for me to dwell in the wild Indian country than in this stockade, where fools accidentally discharge their muskets and others burn down their homes at night."

The fact that the buildings in America's first cities were built mainly of wood meant that fire was a serious threat. Protection was essential and steps were quickly taken to prevent and fight fires. In 1648, Peter Stuyvesant, the governor of New Amsterdam (today's New York) stood on his wooden leg and chose four men to act as fire wardens. The mission of these first

This 1776 drawing depicts a group of men battling a blaze in a colonial town. One man pours water into a wagon, while several pull on a pump and another man aims the hose at the burning building.

fire inspectors was to check all chimneys and make sure none were fire hazards.

Soon after, eight citizens were chosen to make up the Rattle Watch. This patrol roamed New Amsterdam's streets every night. If they spotted a fire, the patrol shook their rattles, waking nearby residents. Under the supervision of the eight citizens, neighbors would form bucket brigades, passing buckets of water from one person to another to douse the fire until it was extinguished. Today, the Rattle Watch is seen as the first example of organized fire fighting in America.

In the 1670s, the city of Boston suffered a series of fires caused by arsonists. The small "ingine," a water pump invented by local ironmaker Joseph Jynks, was no match for these fires. Eventually, the city purchased a high-tech engine that was being used in England at the time. The wooden box that arrived from across the Atlantic—3 feet long and 18 inches wide (1.4 meters by 9 cm)—was equipped with a direct-force pump that fed a small hose. The tublike section of the engine was kept filled with water by a bucket brigade. A captain and twelve men were hired by the city to manage the engine. The "engine company" became America's first. And its captain, Thomas Atkins, was the first fire-fighting officer in the country.

Since early engines could supply only small streams of water, firefighters relied on other equipment for fires that raged out of control. Often, rescue was more of a priority than putting out the flames. Firefighters commonly used a bed key, a small metal tool that helped them quickly take apart the wooden bed frames that were often a family's most valuable possession. Also useful were salvage bags, into which other precious items were tossed and carried out of harm's way.

As new companies were formed, fire fighting became more regulated. One result was the creation of a chain of command with officers who had different levels of authority. Officers were needed to take charge and coordinate the fire-fighting and rescue efforts. In 1711, the city of Boston created the job of fireward. Firewards were given 5-foot (1.52-meter) red staffs topped with shiny brass spikes, which they carried around, to let everyone know who they were.

With experienced leaders in charge, fire companies across the nation became more organized. New equipment and technologies were invented and updated, and fire-fighting techniques became more sophisticated. In the meantime, firefighters themselves were beginning to take on many new tasks. Eventually, the job of firefighter would be about much more than just putting out fires.

Fire Fighting Today

Traditionally, fire fighting has included three main tasks:

1. Preventing fires from breaking out

First Chief

When they hear the name Benjamin Franklin, most people think of the Founding Father who helped draft the Declaration of Independence or the scientist who invented lightning rods and bifocal eyeglasses. Few people know that in 1736, Franklin founded the United States's first volunteer fire company, Philadelphia's Union Fire Company. Because of this, Ben Franklin is considered by many to be the first fire chief in the United States.

2. Preventing fires that do break out from destroying lives and property

3. Containing and then putting out fires

Meanwhile, over the last century, the role of firefighters has branched out in many directions. For example, firefighters are often the first to respond to both minor emergencies and major disasters. They are called upon to help out during earthquakes, hurricanes, plane crashes, building collapses, and terrorist attacks. They are also the first to respond to leaks of gas, water, or hazardous materials; people trapped in elevators or smashed cars; and all sorts of medical emergencies. They frequently receive emergency medical training. An increasing number learn to deal with hazardous materials such as toxic gases or chemicals and are known as HazMat specialists. Many firefighters also receive search and rescue (SAR) training.

SAR

Firefighters have always been involved in rescue work. However, as their responsibilities increased, they began doing more than just pulling people out of burning houses. Other

A group of firemen pose in front of their fire truck in Ithaca, New York, around 1915.

America's First Female Firefighter

The first known female firefighter in the United States was an African American woman named Molly Williams. She went from being a slave to a member of Oceanus Engine Company #11 in New York City. Williams, in her dress and checked apron, was said to be as good a firefighter as many of the men. She was especially helpful during the blizzard of 1818, when she took her place with the men on the ropes and pulled a water pump to a fire through the deep snow.

routine fire-fighting operations soon included rescuing victims in collapsed buildings, flooded rivers, capsized boats, and smashed-up cars. To deal with these different disasters, many fire departments began to develop highly specialized emergency rescue teams. Members of these teams receive special training that allows them to master the growing number of rescue situations, tools, and techniques.

In 1915, the FDNY created Manhattan's Rescue Company 1. Soon after, four other rescue companies were added from Brooklyn, Queens, the Bronx, and Staten Island. During their early years, these pioneer rescue companies responded to a wide variety of disasters both large and small. Aside from putting out fires, they helped out at the sites of collapsed buildings, when there were subway accidents, and at attempted suicides.

The following chapters will explore various aspects of fire fighting. However, special emphasis is placed upon the jobs and lives, equipment, and experiences of firefighters involved in SAR operations.

CHAPTER 2

Climbing the Ladder

Fire fighting is a dangerous profession that isn't for the faint of heart. You need to be very brave and in great physical shape. Constantly dealing with people who are wounded, burned, and in great pain can be emotionally draining. Firefighters frequently come into contact with death and other tragic situations. Working long shifts in often life-threatening situations can be incredibly difficult and stressful. On the upside, saving homes, cities, and human lives can be extraordinarily rewarding.

Firefighters don't work alone. They work in teams. In fact, firefighters don't just work together—they live together. During their long shifts, firefighters train on, clean, and maintain equipment together. They also eat, sleep, and share downtime together at the fire station. The beauty of this is that many firefighters create incredibly strong bonds that last for life. More than just friends, firefighters consider their colleagues to be part of their families. They often refer to each other as brothers and sisters.

Fire-fighting "brothers" survey the damage and search for victims a day after the terrifying events of September 11, 2001.

In fact, there is a long tradition of fire-fighting families in North America. Many male and female firefighters have brothers and sisters, parents, and grandparents who were or are firefighters as well. This intergenerational link was especially devastating during the collapse of the World Trade Center, where many families of FDNY members lost not just one, but two, three, or four relatives. However, the bonds of love and support that exist—between blood and non-blood relatives alike—are unbreakable. Firefighters are always willing to risk their lives to save a colleague. The world saw proof of this during the events of September 11.

Firefighters are also constantly working with the public. Whether educating children, conducting safety inspections, administering first aid, or saving lives, you need a large supply of human compassion and understanding, firmness, patience, and good communication skills to be a good firefighter.

Getting Started

Depending on the state in which you live, you need to be at least eighteen to twenty-one years of age to become a firefighter. However, being a minor doesn't mean you can't start preparing in advance for a fire-fighting career.

Working with local high schools and colleges, some fire departments have set up fire cadet programs. Cadets go through firefighter training and prepare to pass the physical and written

Firefighter trainees go through exercise routines at a training center in Los Angeles, California. Because of the demanding nature of the fire-fighting job, trainees undergo a rigorous training regimen.

exams that are required for all firefighters. Aside from being an invaluable experience, this can be a good way to find out whether fire fighting is truly a career that interests you.

You can do a lot to increase your chances of being recruited by a fire department:

1. Get into shape. You'll need to be in top shape to pass the physical performance test during the hiring process and to do the job once you're part of the department. Try weight lifting, martial arts, or jogging.

2. Do research. Get in touch with neighborhood firefighters to learn about the profession and get some tips. Meanwhile, there are all sorts of books at the library, and fire-fighting magazines are available in print and on the Internet. Be sure to look at the information sections at the back of this book for suggestions.

3. Prepare for the written exam. Your test score on the written exam counts a lot. There are many resources that can provide you with study information and practice exams.

Basic Requirements

Firefighter requirements vary from city to city and county to county. Nevertheless, there are a few basic requirements that all firefighter candidates must meet:

• Residence in the area in which you want to work

- Possession of a valid driver's license

- A high school diploma or equivalent (although some departments have a higher education requirement)

- Good vision

Exams

Assuming that you fulfill the basic requirements, prospective firefighters must pass a series of tests, usually given in the following order:

1. Written exam—multiple choice questions that evaluate reading, math, and problem-solving skills; your knowledge of fire-fighting procedures; and your ability to read maps and floor plans.

2. Personal interview—a review of your personal experiences that evaluates problem-solving, personal relations, and communication skills.

3. Medical exam—a complete physical exam that ensures you can perform all firefighter duties and a psychological test that determines your emotional well-being.

4. Background evaluation—an interview to judge your honesty and respect for the law and for others. This is accompanied by background checks that look at your driving record and criminal record (if you have one).

5. Physical ability test—measures your strength, endurance, and agility. Some of the tasks you will have to carry out include:

- Climbing stairs

- Crawling through a tunnel

- Dragging a hose

- Dragging a human-sized dummy

- Jumping over a wall

- Raising and climbing a ladder

If you meet the basic requirements and breeze through all these tests and exams, you have a good shot at beginning a career as a firefighter. Of course, the more experience and training you have, the better. A certificate or degree in fire science from a college is recommended. In some cases, it is required. And because firefighters must increasingly deal with rescuing victims and administering medical care in emergency situations, emergency medical technician (EMT) training or certification is often necessary.

Career Opportunities

There are currently over 300,000 career firefighters working in the United States. A career firefighter is paid to work full-time.

At the same time, there are approximately one million volunteer firefighters. These reserve firefighters are paid only when they are called to duty. They usually work in small communities or rural areas. Some people start out working as volunteer firefighters in order to gain experience that can help them become career firefighters. Volunteer firefighters either form their own fire companies or work in companies alongside professional firefighters.

Just as the roles and responsibilities of firefighters are constantly expanding, so is the demand for eager and able men and women. Over the next ten years, it is estimated that the nation will need between 5 and 15 percent more firefighters.

The majority of firefighters—90 percent—work for city or county fire departments. However, there are a growing number of other opportunities for firefighters as well. State and federal wildland firefighters specialize in putting out forest fires that rage through state wilderness areas and national parks. They are hired by agencies such as the California Department of Forestry and the U.S. Forest Service. Military firefighters work as firefighters for the U.S. Navy and U.S. Air Force at various military bases and airfields. Private sector firefighters work in areas where fires are particular risks. Airports, ship yards, and oil and chemical refineries all hire their own firefighters, as do large companies that deal with chemicals, oil and gases, or aircraft.

Working Your Way Up the Ladder

Firefighter recruits who are just starting out spend the first one to five years on the job as apprentices. During this time they receive continual training and are constantly tested. The first year—during which recruits are on probation—is a particularly challenging time. If you can't adapt to life as a firefighter, you're out. After the first four months of intensive fire-fighting and EMT training, recruits are assigned to a unit, or company, where they work with experienced firefighters under the supervision of a fire officer.

There are four kinds of fire companies: engine companies, ladder companies, pump companies, and truck companies. Each name is associated with a specific fire-fighting assignment. As such, while some firefighters operate the pumps that release water, others handle ladders or enter burning buildings to rescue survivors.

While on duty, firefighters remain in a state of constant preparation. They must be ready to respond (and their equipment must be in good condition) to any kind of disaster at a moment's notice. When not responding to fires and other emergencies, firefighters have many other jobs to do. They are involved in fire prevention. They also inspect buildings and other areas—airports, chemical waste dumps, and crowded public spaces, for example—to verify that they are not fire risks. Other tasks include enforcing fire regulations and codes (and fining those who break the rules), investigating causes of specific

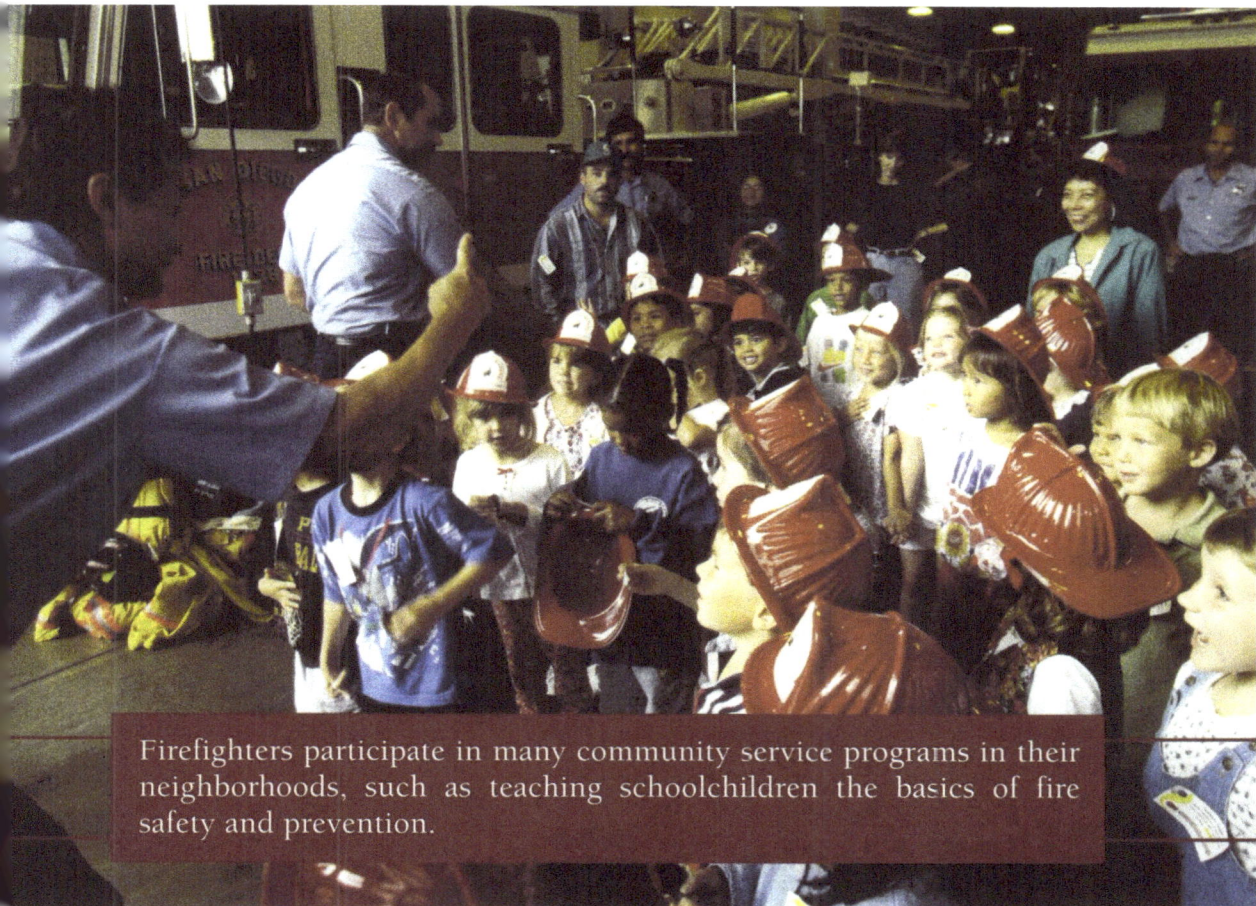

Firefighters participate in many community service programs in their neighborhoods, such as teaching schoolchildren the basics of fire safety and prevention.

fires, and fire education, in which firefighters work with the community, teaching both kids and adults how to prevent fires.

A recruit has many rungs to climb before getting to the top of the ladder. Ongoing training and on-the-job experience can lead to a promotion from level 1 or 2 firefighter to truck driver (which means you get to drive the fire engine). Subsequent promotions are to the level of officers. At this point, you are in charge of directing and organizing other firefighters and rescue operations. After becoming a fire lieutenant, and then a fire captain, you can aim for battalion chief, district chief, deputy chief, assistant fire chief, and—at the top of the ladder—fire chief of an entire department, such as the FDNY.

Rescue Teams

As we saw earlier, technical rescue and disaster response has become a big part of a firefighter's job. Emergency rescue has become a science and a career specialty. Many fire departments have firefighters who are specially trained to deal with various disasters, such as collapsed buildings or floods, just as they have firefighters who are specialists in providing emergency medical services or in dealing with hazardous materials.

Some major departments, such as the FDNY, the Los Angeles Fire Department (LAFD), and the Los Angeles County Fire Department, have even created their own specialized rescue companies whose firefighters are trained and equipped to deal with emergencies and disasters. This new focus on rescue has not only created new strategies but also new knowledge, training, tools, and equipment.

CHAPTER 3

Tools of the Trade

In the early 1700s, the first piece of equipment built specifically for fighting fires was brought to North America. Imported from England, the hand-pumper had a series of long handles that were pumped up and down by volunteers in order to release water from the machine's tub. Although better than bucket brigades, pumping water by hand was pretty exhausting work.

The Little "Engine" That Could...

Today, fire-fighting equipment is a lot more specialized and sophisticated than it was in the early days of combating fires in the United States. Your general "engine company"—the term used to describe the basic throw-water-on-the-fire unit—is a combination of one completely outfitted engine and the crew that operates it. Engines these days can carry up to 500 gallons (1,893 liters) of water and can pump up to 1,500 gallons (5,678 liters) of water

An LAPD firefighter adjusts a dial on an engine to increase the flow of water while battling a fire in the Brentwood Condominiums in Los Angeles, California.

per minute. Rigs are equipped with hoses of various lengths and thickness, as well as nozzles, shutoffs, and other fittings—all of which are stored in special onboard compartments. Vehicles are also stocked with all the necessary protective clothing and breathing equipment required by the crew, which consists of one captain, one engineer, and two firefighters.

Since many firefighters are also emergency medical technicians, vehicles are also outfitted with basic life support tools, such as first-aid kits, medical supplies, oxygen regulators, and automatic defibrillators. Defibrillators use electric shocks to help a stopped heart start beating again. When organized in this manner, one engine and its crew can respond to any kind of emergency—from a car crash or a heart attack victim to a large brush fire or a collapsed building full of trapped people.

The More the Merrier

For major disasters, some fire departments are equipped with more complex fire-fighting teams. For example, the LAFD's task force consists of three different outfits. Accompanying the standard engine company is an aerial truck and a single "pump." Together, the various parts of a task force can take on any disaster.

The pump is a fire engine driven and operated by an engineer. Its main purpose is putting out raging fires. Meanwhile, the aerial truck, staffed by a captain, a truck operator, and three firefighters, is a bit like a hardware store on wheels. It is stocked with multiple ladders that stretch from 12 to 100 feet (3.7 to 30.5 meters) as well as every kind of tool imaginable for breaking into buildings, creating air openings in blocked structures, and doing rescue and salvage work. While the engine company focuses on the water portion of fire fighting, the truck company deals with everything else.

Big Rigs to the Rescue

In recent years, a few fire departments' rescue companies have begun using specially constructed rescue rigs. The LAFD, for example, is proud of its heavy rescue truck known fondly as "the Heavy." The Heavy and its well-trained crew can deal with any kind of rescue emergency and are equipped to take on specific L.A. area disasters such as earthquakes, brush fires, freeway traffic collisions, and floods. Trapped victims can count on this tough rig whose tools allow firefighters to cut, disassemble, and lift all kinds of heavy materials in order to release victims who are trapped.

The Heavy's East Coast equivalent is the FDNY's rescue rig, also known as the Rolling Toolbox because of its incredible assortment of tools and equipment. Aside from regular disasters, New York's rescue companies are equipped to deal with specific New York operations such as people trapped in subway trains and emergencies that take place way at the top of skyscrapers.

New Tools on the Block

High-tech rescue rigs are not the only novelty that firefighters count on for SAR operations. A variety of new tools have been perfected to make rescue missions more efficient.

The Air Source Cart (ASC) is a lightweight portable source of continuous compressed air. It can provide an ongoing supply of air for breathing. It can also furnish a continuous supply of air to operate rescue tools that are powered by compressed air instead of electricity. The ASC is especially useful for emergencies where victims are trapped underwater; in confined, airless spaces; or in areas where hazardous, flammable materials such as gases and oils are present. Rescue tools that are powered by air—known as pneumatic tools—include high-power air drills, saws, and chisels.

To cut victims loose from beneath piles of rubble, rescue companies also rely on special battery-operated saws that can cut through vehicle metal, windshields, and even concrete. These saws are handy in situations where a victim is trapped in a smashed car or a collapsed building, or has a body part stuck in a machine. They are also useful for sawing lumber that can be used to prop—or shore up—the unsteady parts of a collapsed building or structure.

Ropes have been essential rescue tools for a long time. In fact, rope rescue is so important that various fire department rescue teams have special rope rescue and advanced rope rescue

Color Conflict

In the early 1970s, a major scandal erupted among fire departments in the United States. The cause was the introduction of new fire engines that were painted a bright lime green. Supporters argued that since lime green was brighter, the engines would be more visible and thus safer. However, traditionalists stood behind the old red engines.

At one point, there were actually more green trucks being purchased by fire departments than red ones. However, by the 1980s, most fire departments were switching back to red engines, and many green vehicles were being repainted. These days, the lime green fire engine is close to extinction.

training courses. Taking rope rescue a step further is the griphoist, a hand-operated portable machine that can lift and pull wire ropes used for heavy-duty rescue work. A griphoist can raise and lower both light and heavy objects (and people)—up to 6,000 pounds (2,722 kilograms)—in any direction with great ease and precision. It is often used by rescue teams to move large vehicles such as trucks, ships, and cranes that have been involved in accidents, as well as to stabilize loose, hanging, or even burning building parts.

Another rope-related tool—one that has been around for some time—is the Lyle gun. A gadget worthy of Batman or Wonder Woman, the Lyle gun is a .45 caliber line gun with a service cord attached to it. The cord itself is connected to a stronger life-saving rope. Firefighters can shoot the cord to victims trapped in high places or other areas they can't reach. Victims can then clutch onto the life-saving rope and be lifted or pulled to safety.

The FDNY's Brooklyn-based Rescue Company 2 once used the Lyle gun to rescue a child from a vicious dog. The dog had attacked a child previously and continued to be a threat. Firefighters couldn't get close to the child. Instead, they used the Lyle gun to stun the dog and rescue the child.

Members of Rescue 2 also recently developed the "man in machine kit." As its name suggests, this specially assembled tool kit is used to disentangle victims who are stuck or trapped in machines. Tools in the kit include a battery-operated saw, wood and steel wedges, pry bars, a soap solution, and various hand tools such as wrenches, pliers, and screwdrivers. The kit has been used by rescuers to extricate arms caught in dough presses, printing presses, and sheet-folding machines; fingers caught in car gas fill pipes; legs caught in barber chairs; feet caught in bicycle frames; and even a child who was locked in a safe.

Another fairly recent and essential rescue tool is the thermal imaging camera. Because these cameras are heat sensitive, they are ideal for searching for victims trapped beneath rubble. If victims are hidden or unconscious and are unable to cry out, the camera can locate them by detecting their body heat. Thermal cameras are also handy for tracking down lost or disoriented firefighters and for detecting unknown sources of smoke or flames that could break out into a serious fire.

Man's Best Friend

Throughout history, dogs have been used successfully in rescue operations. With their strong senses of smell and hearing, these natural hunters are great at tracking down buried victims who can't be seen by humans. No wonder dogs have become the mascots of many firehouses. Indeed, it is hard to find fire departments that don't employ at least one furry, hard-working, and dependable canine.

Like their human colleagues, rescue dogs have to go through years of training in order to become certified search and rescue (SAR) dogs. Usually, the most talented dogs are natural retriever breeds such as German shepherds and Labrador retrievers. Dogs usually need to start training at a young age—between two and ten months—when they are most obedient.

To become a certified search dog, canines must prove they have the following skills:

- Barking skills—to be able to bark nonstop for thirty seconds, alerting human rescuers that a victim has been found

A rescue dog is transported out of the rubble of the World Trade Center. Many firefighters are trained dog handlers who often work with a canine team during search and rescue operations.

A Bearded Solution

The first firefighters in the United States had to deal with lots of heat, little or no water supply, and the effects of inhaling smoke without any protection. Fire service folklore says that firemen would grow long beards through which they could breathe. The theory was that a fireman would dip his whiskers in a pail of water, then clench his wet beard between his teeth and breathe through his mouth. The wet beard acted as a smoke filter.

- Agility skills—to move without slipping or falling over unsteady debris

- Obedience and comprehension skills—to listen and obey rescuers' commands in the midst of chaotic situations

- Courage and determination—to overcome their natural fears of tunnels, closed spaces, and unstable surfaces

Rescue dogs usually live with firefighters and their families. They are raised as house dogs while they go through training. Once they've received certification, dogs go to work and come home each day with their firefighter handlers. Because they share so much, it's not surprising that many dogs and firefighters become very close.

CHAPTER 4

On the Scene

Being a firefighter is not just a job, it's a way of living. It's a dangerous life, but an exciting and rewarding one as well. Fire fighting is a twenty-four-hour-a-day, 365-days-a-year job. Because the work is nonstop, firefighters work in shifts. Each fire department has its own way of organizing shifts. However, the two most common practices are the twenty-four-hour shift and the split shift.

During twenty-four-hour shifts, firefighters are at the fire station where they are on call for a twenty-four-hour period. After a full day on duty, they receive between forty-eight hours and seventy-two hours of off-duty downtime. On split shifts, firefighters alternate between nine- to ten-hour day shifts and fourteen- to fifteen-hour night shifts. Between shifts, firefighters have between forty-eight and seventy-two hours off. Another popular way of splitting shifts is to divide the day up into three eight-hour periods, with firefighters rotating morning, afternoon, and night shifts every couple of months. Regardless of

Moving through the streets of Boston, Massachusetts, at 3:00 AM, a fire truck speeds to the scene of a huge blaze. Twenty-four hours a day, firefighters are ready to jump into action.

what kind of shift option is chosen, an average firefighter works hard, generally racking up between forty and sixty hours of on-duty time in a week.

Immediate Response

When on the job, firefighters have to be ready to respond immediately to any emergency. When an emergency call comes from the dispatcher, vehicles are completely equipped and ready to ride. On the way to the emergency, sirens are used to warn other traffic to get out of the way. Currently, sirens are electronic, but the earliest vehicles used bells. These were replaced in the 1950s by air horns, which in turn were replaced in the 1960s by mechanical sirens. Recently, some engines have been returning to these mechanical sirens, which are actually louder than the electronic ones.

Once they reach the emergency site, firefighters immediately get to work. If the emergency is a fire, the first step is to hook up the hoses to the fire hydrants. The priority is to aim water at areas in order to best protect trapped victims, while preventing the fire from spreading. The next step is to extinguish the fire altogether.

As soon as it is safe enough, firefighters use both portable and aerial ladders on trucks to gain entrance to burning buildings. They search for and rescue victims while ventilating areas filled with suffocating smoke. They also try to salvage as much valuable property as possible from the flames. Rescued victims receive first aid immediately. If injuries are serious, firefighters who have been trained as emergency medical technicians or paramedics administer aid on the spot. Otherwise, victims are transported to ambulances—some fire departments are equipped with their own—and are accompanied by firefighter paramedics to the closest hospital or clinic for treatment.

Portrait of a Delicate Rescue

Not all rescue operations are quite so straightforward. Many don't even deal with fires. On a September afternoon in

New York City firefighters carry a stretcher covered with the U.S. flag from Ground Zero into a waiting ambulance during a ceremony marking the end of the recovery operations at the site. The empty stretcher represented the close to 1,000 people whose remains were never found.

1998, the Margate Fire Rescue Department in Florida received a call that three workers had been trapped in a trench at an excavation site.

Fire Rescue Unit 118 was the first to arrive on the scene with three firefighter/paramedics. They gave an initial report before being joined by Engine Company 18, which was manned by a lieutenant, a driver, and two more firefighter/paramedics. Realizing that the rescue operation was going to be complicated, the lieutenant called a second fire station for backup.

What made the situation so tricky was that a boulder about the size of a pickup truck and weighing several tons had fallen from one trench wall, pinning the three workers against the opposite wall. One worker had been killed instantly. The other two, Victim 1 and Victim 2, were still alive but trapped.

The victims' legs had been pinned by the boulder. Soil covered one victim up to his waist and the other up to his chest. Rescuers saw that digging the victims out would be very difficult. Three firefighters descended into the trench to see how badly the victims were hurt. They were joined by two paramedics who arrived with the backup rescue unit.

Rescuers began digging through the soil with their hands. But it soon became obvious that freeing the victims would be an even longer and more delicate process than it had initially appeared. Two more fire rescue departments, Broward County and Fort Lauderdale, were asked to send in their technical rescue teams.

41

Broward County's technical rescue team began using lumber to prop up and stabilize the trench and surrounding area. Meanwhile, rescuers inside the trench feared another collapse. They gathered anything they could find from the construction site to shore up the trench walls. Margate's firefighters were in charge of giving medical care to the victims. Two paramedics stayed in the trenches and provided advanced life support, including intravenous fluids and oxygen. It was a challenge to keep the victims' air passages open since they kept vomiting blood. While the victims were being treated, a second collapse suddenly occurred, injuring one of the rescuers.

While all this was taking place, a lieutenant from the Fort Lauderdale rescue team remembered that a confined spaces rescue class was being taught at a fire academy in the Fort Lauderdale area. He contacted the class instructors, who arrived soon after with the fire academy's fully equipped heavy rescue rig.

All of this backup was essential. Aside from being pinned by the boulder and buried in soil, Victim 1's leg was pinned against a metal stake. And to keep the trench from filling up with groundwater, rescuers had to use "dewatering" equipment. Air chisels were used to chip away at the boulder, and other air tools were used to remove dirt and rocks from around the victims' lower bodies. Tools had to be operated beneath the surface of the mud and water so that the victims wouldn't be further injured. Yet, if they were operated too far beneath the surface, there was the danger of puncturing the sewer pipe located at the bottom, which would release raw sewage into the trench.

After three hours, Victim 1 was rescued and transported by helicopter to a trauma center. Victim 2 was in very bad shape. Paramedics contacted the trauma center via radio and received permission to give him blood as a treatment for "crush syndrome." Crush syndrome occurs when a part of the body is trapped for a long time, keeping blood from circulating to the area. The blood in the "crushed" limbs fills with deadly poisons that, when freed, can cause cardiac arrest.

Luckily, an hour later, Victim 2 was successfully treated, rescued, and flown to the trauma center. Afterward, the dead worker's body was sent to the medical examiner's office. Then all rescue workers were decontaminated. Many had been exposed to dirt, chemicals, and victims' blood and fluids, any of which could have led to infections or diseases. All firefighters and rescue workers then held a debriefing, during which they discussed the operation. They discussed which rescue strategies had worked and which hadn't. By that time, it was almost midnight. Seven hours had passed since Margate's fire department received the initial call. It had been a long, stressful, but ultimately successful day.

CHAPTER 5

Heroes

After fighting a grass fire that was started by an elderly lady who wasn't watching her burn pile, [the woman] approached us and said thank you and asked how much this was going to cost her. She pulled out her checkbook and added, "I hope it's not more than $300 or I'll have to postdate it for the first of the month." We all smiled and explained that's what her taxes covered. With a bewildered look on her face she said, "Well, I would rather pay it now because I'm always broke after I pay my taxes and can't afford the extra money." Then we laughed and told her it was on us this time. The following week, we had fresh chocolate chip cookies at the station with a note: "To my heroes: a cookie with a kiss."

—Anonymous firefighter
(Source: Fire & EMS Information Network's True Stories Web page, http://www.fire-ems.net)

Perhaps no other profession comes closer to defining heroism than fire fighting. Images of men and women entering burning

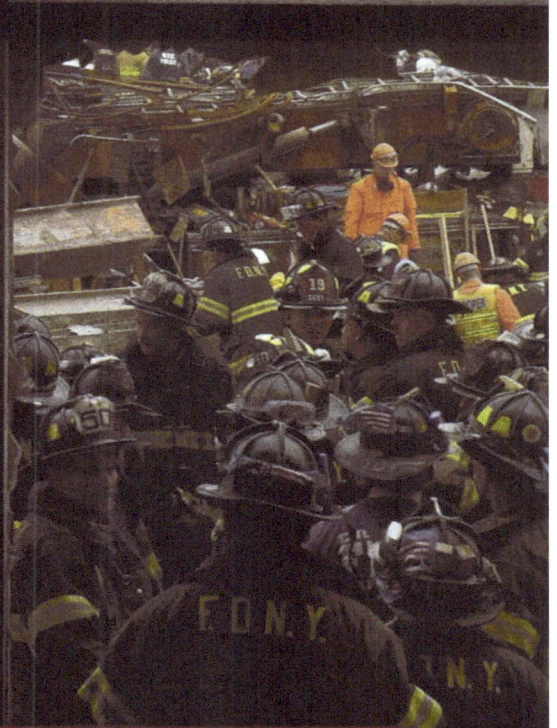

For more than eight months, firefighters worked long shifts trying to recover the remains of people who were killed in the terrorist strikes against the World Trade Center. Many of these heroes refused to take recommended time off, despite the physically and emotionally grueling demands of the recovery effort.

buildings, risking their own lives to save the lives of strangers, are common. We see these images in magazines and newspapers, in films, and on TV and the Internet. We see them daily—all over the world.

Firefighters display heroism in such moments. Putting out a neighborhood fire is heroic. So is bravely entering two burning skyscrapers that have been hit by a pair of hijacked airplanes, battling heat, smoke, fear, panic, and horror—all because of a commitment to save lives. What is it like to be involved in such a rescue effort? The following are some first-person impressions of the September 11 rescue efforts by New York firefighters.

Calling All Units…

FDNY firefighter John Lightsey was working as a radio dispatcher in Manhattan on the morning of September 11. He helped to decide which fire units to send to the emergency.

As soon as he heard the news of the attacks, he dispatched every company from 125th Street down to the World Trade Center. Everybody on the west side was sent to 1 World Trade Center, while everybody on the east side was sent to 2 World Trade Center. All firefighters were instructed to bring every piece of equipment they had in their quarters.

"I knew I had the biggest event in my life when those towers came down," recalls Lightsey. "No one would ever, ever even dream about something like that…"

For Lightsey, the worst was the complete silence after the collapse. For at least fifteen or twenty minutes there was dead air over all radios. Lightsey tried to contact many different companies, but nobody responded. He kept trying and trying.

"I get teary eyed because of the people I knew who we sent down there," Lightsey confesses. "Just thinking about them being down there. Or feeling guilt about assigning all those companies at the same time. We didn't follow the rules; we went above the rules. We went ahead and assigned more than was necessary because of the instinct. A chief, Joe DeBernardo, told me, 'You have to look at it this way. You are not going to stop a firefighter from going in,' and he said, 'what you guys did down there in sending as much man-power as you did, you ended up saving a lot more lives than what they lost.'"

(Source: Dennis Smith. *Report from Ground Zero*. Viking, 2002.)

First on the Scene

FDNY firefighter Maureen B. McArdle Schulman was at Engine Company 35—her firehouse for almost twenty years—when the call came about a plane flying into the World Trade Center. She immediately headed down to the disaster site.

Between 75 and 100 firefighters were at the command center waiting for assignments into one of the towers. Some fire companies came out, and others went in to relieve them. Suddenly, someone shouted out that something was falling from one of the towers. It was one of the 150 people who either decided to jump or were blown out of Tower 1.

"It was a horrific scene," McArdle Schulman remembers. "We stared, in disbelief, or maybe in shock. A few of us turned away and stared at the wall, but we could still hear the bodies hit . . . How horrible could it have been up there, if it made people jump knowing they were going to die?"

McArdle Schulman recalls suddenly seeing a ring of fire at the top of Tower 2. The whole building immediately began puffing up and vibrating. Then the building came down.

"Everyone was running ahead of me," says McArdle Schulman. "I stayed behind, afraid I would be crushed and even more afraid I would lose my sense of direction. At the same time, I was wondering if there would be a secondary explosion in the garage or if the entrance to the garage would collapse, trapping us … I couldn't breathe: The air was thick with dust and we don't know what else. It was dark all around us. I put my face piece on; it was full of dust, too. All the dust went into my mouth and my eyes. My eyes were on fire."

(Source: Maureen B. McArdle Schulman. "Into the Bowels of Hell." *Firework*, March 2002.)

One of Many Fire-Fighting Legends

Captain Patrick Brown was something of an FDNY legend. He had movie-star good looks and spent twenty-three years performing death-defying acts of courage that were often described in the newspapers. He didn't mind risking his life on the job because it was his job as a firefighter that had helped save him from falling into severe depression when he returned from fighting the Vietnam War in the 1970s.

On September 11, Brown and eleven of his firefighters from Ladder Company 3 entered the north tower of the World Trade Center. They were in the midst of a rescue operation on the fortieth floor when the entire tower collapsed.

In his spare time, Brown ran marathons, taught karate to the blind, and practiced yoga. Thousands gathered for the High Mass given in his honor at New York's St. Patrick's Cathedral on what would have been the firefighter's forty-ninth birthday.

The Day After

On September 11, Brenda Berkman, lieutenant of Ladder Co. 12 in midtown Manhattan, had the day off. However, as soon as she heard that a plane had crashed into the World Trade

Center, she got into her uniform and hurried to lower Manhattan, where she remained for two days.

On the second day, rescue workers began to excavate. Although a few cranes were used, because rescuers still hoped to find survivors, most digging was done by hand. Berkman remembers that the rubble piles "went up about twenty feet [six meters], then went down three stories, then went up about seven stories, and on the other side of that they said the pit was about ten stories down."

Working conditions at Ground Zero were extremely dangerous. Still-burning fires created lots of heat and smoke. In the meantime, rescuers were working on very shaky rubble that consisted mainly of jagged metal and rebar. Dust was everywhere. Injuries among rescuers were a constant threat. While moving a piece of metal, Berkman cut open her arm and sliced her hand. However, like many others, and regardless of her injuries, she returned to work after being bandaged by a paramedic.

Workers on the rubble pile lost all sense of time. "When we were down there for twelve hours, it seemed like we were down there for two hours," recalls Berkman. "The only way you could tell time was you just got so exhausted you couldn't stand up anymore."

It took Berkman and other rescuers six hours to climb to the top of a seven-story rubble pile. They worked their way up a line of people that were lining ladders as if composing a human handrail. Anyone who fell off the ladders that were the pathway up would fall and end up cut to pieces or trapped in a hole. Supplies and equipment were passed up and down the line in large buckets. "We'd call for water and bottled water would come by," says Berkman. "Every once in a while, food would come by. We were eating cold hot dogs out of these buckets, sandwiches made by prisoners upstate." From the top of the pile, bodies were passed back down.

(Source: Linda F. Willing. "Report from Ground Zero: The World Trade Center Collapse." *Firework*, September 2001.)

Following the terrorist attacks of September 11, New York City, the United States, and the world rediscovered the heroism of firefighters. The sacrifices they make every day were tragically underscored by the lives of the 343 firefighters who perished in the World Trade Center.

During the weeks that firefighters steadfastly continued rescue operations at Ground Zero, citizens provided them with food, clothing, bedding, and other needed supplies. New Yorkers lined the streets daily to cheer the firefighters as they traveled from Ground Zero to makeshift shelters or fire stations for a few hours of sleep before working yet another twenty-four-hour shift. Months later, fire stations throughout New York City were still being flooded with flowers and food, and cards and letters of thanks and admiration.

Memorial Beam

On April 22, 2002, a New York firefighter at Ground Zero was seen spray painting "E54" and "L4" on a steel beam. The codes referred to Engine Company 54 and Ladder Company 4—fire companies that participated in the World Trade Center rescue operations. The beam itself was the last remaining support beam from the World Trade Center's collapsed south tower. The beam became a memorial to the rescue workers and civilians who lost their lives. It was scheduled to be the last remnant removed from Ground Zero.

Millions of dollars were raised for fire stations and for the families of firefighters who died at the World Trade Center. The U.S. Senate unanimously passed a motion giving medals of bravery to firefighters and other public safety workers. Books paying tribute to the firefighters' bravery were published. Documentaries were made and broadcast on television. Meanwhile, on the streets of New York and other cities, street vendors peddled FDNY caps, sweatshirts, mugs, and other firefighter paraphernalia.

In April 2002, President George W. Bush hosted a dinner for national fire and emergency services in Washington, D.C. During the dinner, he made the following speech to his guests: "Yours is one of the highest callings in our country, and one of the hardest. Your neighborhoods depend on you and so does your country. And you never let us down…We know there will always be fires and someone will have to face the flames. America will always be dependent on people for that work. There is no substitute for the raw courage of the firefighter."

GLOSSARY

agile Physically quick and well-coordinated.

air horn An early fire siren.

arsonist Someone who burns property on purpose or for criminal reasons.

canine A dog.

debriefing A session in which a specialist questions someone about a just-finished job or mission.

debris The remains of something that was destroyed.

defibrillator A medical device that uses electric shocks to help a person's stopped heart start beating.

dispatcher A person who sends others on assignments.

extricate To remove, or pull out.

ground zero The center or point of origin of an intense or violent activity.

hazardous Dangerous.

paramedic A medic trained to deal with medical emergencies and the transportation of emergency victims.

pneumatic tool A tool powered by compressed air.

probation A trial or testing period.

rebar Steel rods with ridges used as support in concrete.

rigging A network of structures used to prop up, secure, and stabilize parts of a collapsed building.

rubble Broken fragments of a building.

salvage To rescue something from being destroyed.

shore up To prop up using structures assembled from lumber.

staff A rod carried as a symbol of authority.

toxic Poisonous.

trench A long, narrow cut in the ground or dirt.

FOR MORE INFORMATION

International Association of Fire Fighters (IAFF)
1750 New York Avenue NW
Washington, DC 20006
(202) 737-8484
Web site: http://www.iaff.org

Los Angeles County Fire Department
1320 N. Eastern Avenue
Los Angeles, CA 90063
(323) 881-2413
Web site: http://www.lacofd.org

Los Angeles Fire Department
200 North Main Street
Los Angeles, CA 90012
(213) 485-5971
Web site: http://www.lafd.org

National Fire Protection Association
1 Batterymarch Park
P.O. Box 9101
Quincy, MA 02269-9101
(617) 770-3000
Web site: http://www.nfpa.org

New York City Fire Museum
278 Spring Street
New York, NY 10013
(212) 691-1303
Web site: http://www.nycfiremuseum.org

United States Fire Administration (USFA)
16825 S. Seton Avenue
Emmitsburg, MD 21727
(301) 447-1000
Web site: http://www.usfa.fema.gov

Women in the Fire Service, Inc.
P.O. Box 5446
Madison, WI 53705
(608) 233-4768
Web site: http://www.wfsi.org

Web Sites

Due to the changing nature of Internet links, the Rosen Publishing Group, Inc., has developed an online list of Web sites related to the subject of this book. This site is updated regularly. Please use this link to access the list:

http://www.rosenlinks.com/csro/fdsr/

FOR FURTHER READING

Braunworth, Brent. *Blood, Guts and Tears: A Firefighter Shares Stories of Courage*. Lanham, MD: National Book Network, 2000.

McGillian, Jamie Kyle, and Jake Miller. *On the Job with a Firefighter: Neighborhood Guardian*. Hauppauge, NY: Barrons Juveniles, 2001.

Oleksy, Walter G. *Choosing a Career as a Firefighter*. New York: The Rosen Publishing Group, Inc., 2000.

Schomp, Virginia. *If You Were a Firefighter*. Windsor, ON: Benchmark Books, 1998.

Smith, Dennis. *Report from Ground Zero: The Story of the Rescue Efforts at the World Trade Center*. New York: Viking Press, 2002.

BIBLIOGRAPHY

Accardi, Russell T. "Specialized Rescue: Excavation Crew Pinned in Trench." *Firehouse Magazine*, September 1998. Retrieved May 8, 2002 (http://www.firehouse.com/magazine/archives/1998/September/specializedrescue.html).

"The American Fire Service: 1648–1998." *FireHouse Magazine*, September 1998. Retrieved May 9, 2002 (http://www.firehouse.com/magazine/american/).

City of New York—Fire Department. "History of Manhattan Fire Companies." Retrieved May 12, 2002 (http://www.ci.nyc.ny.us/html/fdny/html/home2.html).

Downey, Tom. "A Voice from the Rubble." *New York Times Magazine*, September 23, 2001 (republished on FDNY Web site). Retrieved May 10, 2002 (http://www.fdnyrescue2.com/rescue2pics2.html).

The Fire & EMS (Emergency Medical Services) Information Network. Retrieved May 13, 2002 (http://www.fire-ems.net).

Firefighter's Handbook: Essentials of Fire Fighting and Emergency Response. Clifton Park, NY: Delmar Publishers, 2000.

Gaskell, Stephanie. "9-11 Tape Show Firefighters' Courage." Associated Press. February 18, 2002 (republished on

Firehouse.com Web site). Retrieved May 10, 2002
    (http://www.firehouse.com/news/2002/2/18_APtape.html).

Hashagen, Paul. "Fire Fighting in Colonial America." *Firehouse*
    Magazine. Retrieved May 7, 2002 (http://www.firehouse.com/
    magazine/american/colonial.html).

Los Angeles County Fire Department. "Hot Topics," "Services," "Facts
    and Stats," and "News and Media." Retrieved May 10, 2002
    (http://www.lacofd.org/).

Los Angeles Fire Department (LAFD). "General Information,"
    "Firefighter Recruitment Information," and "In-Service
    Training." Retrieved May 10, 2002 (http://www.lafd.org/).

McArdle Schulman, Maureen B. "Into the Bowels of Hell." *Firework*,
    March 2002. Retrieved May 11, 2002 (http://www.wfsi.org/
    SchulmanWTC.html).

Murtagh, James J. *Firefighters' Exams* (Barrons' Firefighters Exams,
    4th ed.). Haupaugge, NY: Barrons, 2000.

Smith, Dennis. *Report from Ground Zero: The Story of the Rescue*
    Efforts at the World Trade Center. New York: Viking Press, 2002.

Willing, Linda F. "Report from Ground Zero: The World Trade
    Center Collapse." *Firework*, September 2001. Retrieved May 11,
    2002 (http://www.wfsi.org/BerkmanWTC.html).

Women in the Fire Service, Inc. "News" and "Info/Statistics."
    Retrieved May 13, 2002 (http://www.wfsi.org).

INDEX

About the Author

Mitchell Fall is a journalist and part-time chef.

Photo Credits

Cover, p. 52 © Mike Segar/TimePix; pp. 1, 35, 45 © TimePix; p. 5 © Jeff Christensen/TimePix; p. 6 © Peter Morgan/TimePix; pp. 9, 13, 14 © Hulton/Archive/Getty Images; p. 17 © Shannon Stapleton/TimePix; p. 19 © Layne Kennedy/Corbis; p. 25 © IndexStock; p. 28 © Joseph Sohm/Corbis; p. 38 © George Hall/Corbis; p. 40 © Corbis.

Editor

Annie Sommers

Designer

Nelson Sá

www.ingramcontent.com/pod-product-compliance
Lightning Source LLC
Chambersburg PA
CBHW061152030426
42336CB00002B/22